Who's Who & What's What in the Bible

a Bible reference handbook

H. J. Richards

Kevin Mayhew

First published in 1999 by
KEVIN MAYHEW LTD
Buxhall
Stowmarket
Suffolk IP14 3DJ

0 1 2 3 4 5 6 7 8 9

ISBN 1 84003 366 5
Catalogue No 1500269

Cover design by Jaquetta Sergeant
Typesetting by Richard Weaver
Printed and bound in Great Britain

CONTENTS

'When I pray, I pray quickly because I'm talking to God.
But when I read the Bible, I read slowly because God's talking to me.'

FOREWORD

This book contains nothing new. The information it provides may be found in countless encyclopaedias, biblical handbooks and introductions to Scripture.

But not easily found. This book is for those who need to know, at a moment's notice, where and in which Gospel such and such a parable of Jesus is told. Or miracle. Or how many centimetres there are in a cubit, or litres in a measure, or pounds in a talent. Or the approximate date of the Books of Samuel, and what was going on in the biblical world at that time.

There are also a number of lists designed for quick consultation: the Commandments, the Beatitudes, the tribes of Israel, Jewish feasts, English translations of the Bible, and so on. And a few maps for orientation.

Those who will perhaps thank me most for this handbook are:

- RE teachers needing to set projects and group work on biblical material. This book in the class library could be a lifesaver.

- Those courageous souls who volunteer to read from the lectern at church services. The last pages of this book contain a pronunciation guide for the 400 or so proper names they might encounter. To such readers I say what one of the great Old Testament teachers said: 'My soul will rejoice (from *Aaron* AIR-on to *Zipporah* ZIP-or-a) when your lips speak what is right.' (*Proverbs 23:16*)

H. J. RICHARDS

SECTION ONE: THE OLD TESTAMENT

1. Contents of the Old Testament

The contents page of many Bibles sets out the books of the Old Testament in four groups: legal books, historical books, doctrinal books and prophetical books.

This grouping was only adopted in the thirteenth century. The Jews have always divided their Bible quite differently into three, reflecting the order in which the three groups of books were formed. They call these three groups *The Law, The Prophets* and *The Writings.*

The Law contains the basic teaching (in Hebrew *Torah*) by which Moses believed that God wanted his people to live. The teaching lies both in the stories of Israel's origins, and in its legislation. The Greeks called these five volumes the *Penta*-teuch:

> Genesis
> Exodus
> Leviticus
> Numbers
> Deuteronomy

The Prophets is the title of the collected preaching of the prophets, prefaced by their interpretation of the events through which they lived. These are divided into *former* and *latter* prophets.

Former prophets	Latter prophets
Joshua	Isaiah
Judges	Jeremiah
1 Samuel	Ezekiel
2 Samuel	Hosea
1 Kings	Joel
2 Kings	Amos
	Obadiah
	Jonah
	Micah
	Nahum
	Habakkuk
	Zephaniah
	Haggai
	Zechariah
	Malachi

The Writings comprise the miscellaneous sacred writings which were the last to be formed into a collection, some so late that they were eventually excluded from some translations of the Bible.

Psalms	*Deutero-canonical* or *Apocryphal*
Proverbs	Baruch
Job	Judith
Song of songs	Tobit
Ruth	Ecclesiasticus
Lamentations	Wisdom
Ecclesiastes	1 Maccabees
Esther	2 Maccabees
Daniel	Some additions to the books of Esther and Daniel
Ezra	
Nehemiah	
1 Chronicles	
2 Chronicles	

The Bible was not divided into chapters until the thirteenth century, by the Archbishop of Canterbury Stephen Langton. The further division into verses was largely done in the sixteenth century by the Parisian printer Robert Estienne, who is said to have marked off the verses as he rode on horseback between Paris and Geneva. Before these 'modern' aids were invented, anyone wishing to give a reference could only say, 'In the book of Deuteronomy (Isaiah, Matthew and so on) it says . . .'

2. Dates of the Old Testament books

Books of the Bible	History of Israel	Contemporary events	Date BCE
Genesis 12-50	Patriarchs migrate into Palestine	Middle East invaded by Amorites	2000
		Egyptian rule in Palestine	
	Migration to Egypt	Hyksos kings in Egypt	1500
	Slavery in Egypt		
Narratives of Exodus and Numbers	Escape from Egypt under Moses	Egypt vs Hittites in Palestine	1300
	Mount Sinai		
Joshua	Occupation of Palestine	End of Hittite power	
Judges	Struggle for independence, especially against Philistines	Philistines invade Palestine	1200
1 Samuel	Saul anointed king	End of Egyptian power	1100
2 Samuel	King David	End of Philistine power	1000
Some psalms	Israel's Golden Age	Assyrian Empire established	
Genesis 2-11	First writing of patriarchal traditions		
1 Kings	Solomon		
	Schism of Kingdom into north (Israel) and south (Judah)		
2 Kings	Elijah and Elisha	Assyria extends Empire south	900
Amos			800
Hosea	Israel crushed by Assyria and exiled	Rome founded	
Isaiah 1-39, Micah	Judah threatened		700
Deuteronomy	Josiah's religious reform in Judah		
	Publication of 'Deuteronomic History' (Joshua-Judges-Samuel-Kings)		
Nahum		End of Assyrian Empire	
Zephaniah			
Jeremiah		Rise of Babylon	600
Ezekiel	First exiles to Babylonia		597
	Jerusalem destroyed		586
	Babylonian exile		
Isaiah 40-55			
Habakkuk	Discussion of problem of evil		
Proverbs, Job, Leviticus	Codification of Law		
Laws in Exodus and Numbers	Priests assume leadership		
Genesis 1			
Haggai	Return of exiles to Jerusalem	Persia rules Middle East	
Zechariah 1-8			
Some psalms	Building of second Temple		
	Break with Samaria	Roman Republic established	500
Ezra-Nehemiah	Jerusalem rebuilt	Golden Age of Greece	
Chronicles			

Malachi, Joel	Reform movements		400
Obadiah			
Isaiah 56-66			
Ruth, Jonah		Persia defeated by Alexander	
		Greek Empire declines	
Zechariah 9-14	End of prophetical	Rise of Roman power	300
	movement	Roman wars with Carthage	
Tobit, Ecclesiasticus	Greek influence		200
Ecclesiastes			
Song of Songs			
Daniel	Maccabee revolt		
1 and 2 Maccabees	Jewish independence	End of Greek Empire	
Judith, Esther			
Wisdom		Rome rules the world	
	Dead Sea Scrolls	Gallic Wars	100
	Herod the Great	Pompey and Caesar	
		Augustus, first Emperor	

The Bishops' Bible of 1568 became known as the Breeches Bible *because of its translation of the clothes that Adam and Eve made for themselves out of fig leaves in Genesis 3:7.*

3. Kings of Israel and Judah

		BCE
	Saul	1030
	David	1010
	Solomon	970

Judah			Israel	
Rehoboam	931		Jeroboam I	931
Abijam	913		Nadab	910
Asa	911			
			Baasha	909
			Elah	886
			Zimri	885
			Omri	885
Jehoshaphat	870		Ahab	874
Jehoram (Joram)	848		Ahaziah	853
Ahaziah	841		Jehoram	852
Athaliah	841		Jehu	841
Joash (Jehoash)	835		Jehoahaz	814
Amaziah	796		Joash	798
Uzziah (Azariah)	781		Jeroboam II	783
			Zechariah	743
			Shallum	743
Jotham	740		Menahem	743
Ahaz	736		Pekahiah	738
			Pekah	737
			Hoshea	732
			(Fall of Samaria	721)
Hezekiah	716			
Manasseh	687			
Amon	642			
Josiah	640			
Jehoahaz	609			
Jehoiakim	609			
Jehoiachin	598			
Zedekiah	597			
(Fall of Jerusalem	586)			

William Tyndale's footnote to the text of Numbers 23:8, 'How shall I curse whom God curses not?', is 'The Pope can tell how'.

4. Numbering of the Psalms

The numbering of the Psalms in most Bibles and reference books is taken from the Hebrew text of the Old Testament. This differs from the numbering followed by the early Greek translation called the *Septuagint* on which older Catholic translations (for example the Douay Version) were based. The following table illustrates the difference:

Hebrew numbers	Greek (Catholic) numbers
1-8	1-8
9-10	9
11-113	10-112
114-115	113
116	114-115
117-146	116-145
147	146-147
148-150	148-150

In short, for most of the psalms, the generally accepted Hebrew numbering is one ahead of the Greek (and Catholic) numbering.

Verse numbers are also occasionally different. When a psalm has a long title, this is counted as the first verse (and sometimes even the second verse) in some older translations. More recent translations begin verse numbers with the actual text of the psalm. The opening of the famous *Miserere*, for example, 'Have mercy on me, O God, according to thy steadfast love', is numbered Psalm 50:3 in the Douay Version, and Psalm 51:1 in the Revised Standard Version.

Since the 46th word of Psalm 46 (Authorised Version 1611) is 'shake' and the word 'spear' appears shortly after, some people are convinced that the psalm was translated by William Shakespeare (died 1616).

The printers of a seventeenth-century Bible were fined £3,000 for substituting 'a' for 'no' in the opening line of Psalm 14: 'The fool hath said in his heart there is a God.'

5. Biblical feasts and festivals

The basic Old Testament calendar celebrates three agricultural feasts during the year:

Pesach (Passover) at the beginning of April marks the birth of the spring lambs. Roast lamb is eaten with unleavened bread from the early corn. Since the Exodus from Egypt took place during this festival, Passover became the most important ceremony of the year.

Shevuot (Pentecost) celebrates both the grain harvest fifty days later towards the end of May, and the receiving of the Law by Moses at Mount Sinai.

Sukkot (Tabernacles) marks the end of the fruit harvest at the beginning of October. Tabernacles (tents) are erected outdoors to recall both the harvest and the Exodus journey through the desert.

Later three more feasts were interwoven with these:

Purim is mentioned only in the book of Esther, and is another celebration of deliverance, this time from slavery in Persia. It is kept at the beginning of March, in a carnival atmosphere.

Yom Kippur (Atonement) is a solemn celebration of penance and reconciliation in mid-October, when those who are estranged from God by sin are again made 'at one' with him.

Hanukkah (Dedication) in December commemorates the rededication of the Jerusalem Temple after its desecration in Maccabee times. It is a feast of lights, and has become for some an occasion for Jews and Christians to celebrate mid-winter together.

The weekly *Sabbath* or rest day, like most biblical feasts, has overtones of the Exodus: even slaves should be given a regular day off. Its observance, like that of the Christian Sunday, has at times become oppressive, but its essence has always been a liberating one – to provide rest, recreation and joy.

When the comedian W. C. Fields was on his deathbed in 1946, he was asked why he kept riffling through his Bible. He replied, 'I'm looking for loopholes'.

SECTION TWO: THE NEW TESTAMENT

1. Contents of the New Testament

Many New Testaments divide their contents into three groups: historical (Gospels and Acts); doctrinal (Epistles); prophetical (Book of Revelation). In actual fact the books fall more naturally into four groups:

The Good News of the Gospel. Three parallel presentations by:

> Mark
> Matthew
> Luke

Most scholars agree that the present Gospels of Matthew and Luke are later than the Gospel of Mark, which they have used as a source. The three are known as the 'look-alike' (Greek *synoptic*) Gospels.

The Pauline Collection. Luke's Gospel continues into a second volume, to provide a background for the work of Paul and his disciples, and their correspondence with the Christian communities founded by Paul.

Acts of the Apostles	Colossians
1 Thessalonians	Philemon
2 Thessalonians	Ephesians
1 Corinthians	1 Timothy
2 Corinthians	2 Timothy
Philippians	Titus
Galatians	Hebrews
Romans	

The General Epistles. Letters written by other early Christian leaders to the Church at large:

> James
> 1 Peter
> Jude
> 2 Peter

The Johannine Collection. John and his disciples tell the Good News of what Jesus has come to mean to those who have known him for a long time:

> John's Gospel
> Three Epistles of John
> Book of Revelation

The shortest verse in the Bible is John 11:35: 'Jesus wept.'

---

2. Dates of the New Testament books

Books of the Bible	Events in Palestine	Events outside	Date BCE
	Birth of Jesus	Augustus Emperor	6
	Death of Herod the Great		4
	Archelaus rules in Judaea		
	Herod Antipas rules in Galilee		CE
	Judaea under Roman rule		6
		Tiberius Emperor	14
	Pontius Pilate governor		26
	John the Baptist		
	Ministry of Jesus		
	Death of Jesus		30
	Conversion of Paul		36
	Mission to Samaria	Caligula Emperor	37
	Herod Agrippa rules Judaea	Claudius Emperor	41
	Paul's first journey		45
	Council of Jerusalem		
First written records of Jesus	Paul's second journey		49
James			
1 Thessalonians			50
2 Thessalonians			51
	Paul's third journey based on		53
	Ephesus	Nero Emperor	54
1 Corinthians			56
2 Corinthians			57
Philippians			
Galatians	Paul in Corinth		
Romans			
	Paul in prison		58
	Paul sent to Rome		60
Colossians			
Philemon			
Ephesians?			
Mark		Persecution of Christians in Rome	65
1 Peter		Martyrdom of Peter	
1 Timothy			66
2 Timothy			
Titus			
	Jewish War of Independence	Martyrdom of Paul	67
Hebrews		Galba Emperor	68
		Vespasian Emperor	69
	Destruction of Jerusalem		70
	Fall of Masada		73
Matthew			75
Jude		Titus Emperor	79
		Domitian Emperor	81
Luke			85
Acts			
Revelation		Persecution of Christians	95
John			
Epistles of John		Nerva Emperor	96
2 Peter			

3. The Herod family

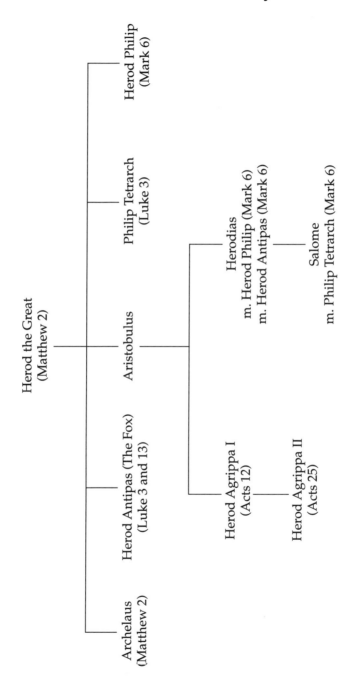

4. Miracles in the Gospels

The miracle stories of the Gospels illustrate the rule of God (Kingdom) being established by Christ in a godless world. Christ is shown as:

Liberating the human race from the forces of evil

	Mark	Matthew	Luke	John
Man possessed	1:23		4:33	
Many possessed	1:32, 3:11	8:16	4:40, 6:18	
Legion	5:1ff	8:28ff	8:26ff	
Dumb demon		9:32, 12:22	11:14	
Possessed girl	7:24ff	15:21ff		
Possessed boy	9:17ff	17:14ff	9:37ff	
Blind and dumb demon		12:22		

Healing the wounded

	Mark	Matthew	Luke	John
Simon's mother-in-law	1:30-31	8:14-15	4:38-39	
Leper	1:40ff	8:2ff	5:12ff	
Paralytic	2:3ff	9:2	5:18ff	
Withered hand	3:1ff	12:9ff	6:6ff	
Many sick	3:10	4:23, 12:15	6:18	
Centurion's servant		8:5ff	7:1ff	4:46ff
Two blind men		9:27ff		
Bleeding woman	5:25ff	9:20ff	8:43ff	
Many sick	6:56	9:35, 14:35, 15:30		
Deaf mute	7:32ff			
Blind man	8:22ff			
Blind Bartimaeus	10:46ff	20:29ff	18:35ff	
Crippled woman			13:11ff	
Man with dropsy			14:2ff	
Ten lepers			17:12ff	
Malchus' ear			22:51	
Cripple at Bethzatha				5:1ff
Man born blind				9:1ff

Providing life abundant

	Mark	Matthew	Luke	John
Water into wine				2:1ff
Feeding of thousands	6:31ff, 8:1ff	14:15ff, 15:32ff	9:12ff	6:5ff
Draught of fishes			5:4ff	21:1ff

Conquering even the power of death

	Mark	Matthew	Luke	John
The raging sea	4:36ff	8:23ff	8:22ff	
Widow's son raised			7:11ff	
Jairus' daughter raised	5:22ff	9:18ff	8:41ff	
The waters of death	6:45ff	14:22ff		6:16ff
Lazarus raised				11:1ff

An 1810 edition of the Bible recommended the reader to hate his own 'wife' instead of 'life', in Luke 14:26.

Note:

The Acts of the Apostles, which is in effect the second volume of Luke's gospel, tells of the disciples of Jesus continuing his work in the following miracle stories:

	Acts
Lame man	3:1ff
Many sick	5:12
Stephen	6:8ff
Philip	8:13
Aeneas healed	9:32ff
Tabitha raised	9:36ff
Paul and Barnabas	14:3
Cripple at Lystra	14:8ff
Possessed girl	16:16ff
Paul at Ephesus	19:11-12
Paul in Malta	28:8-9

The headline of a Jerusalem newspaper in the year CE 30:
Lazarus Obituary: A Correction

---

5. Parables in the Gospels

According to the New Testament, the Rule of God (Kingdom) is imminent. It will be not only a gift from God, but surprisingly different from what people may expect, and a challenge to all.

A gift from God

	Mark	Matthew	Luke
Doctor healing the sick	2:17	9:12	5:31
Pardoned debtor			7:41ff
Abundant harvest	4:3ff	13:3ff	8:5ff
City on display		5:14	
Shining light	4:21	5:15	8:16, 11:33
Treasure kept safe		6:19ff	12:33
Hungry child fed		7:9	11:11
Treasure trove		13:44	
Rare pearl		13:45	
Lost sheep found		18:12ff	15:4ff
Lost coin found			15:8ff
Lost son found (Prodigal)			15:11ff
Flowering fig tree	13:28	24:32	21:29-30

A surprise

	Mark	Matthew	Luke
Feasting not fasting	2:18ff	9:15	5:33ff
New clothes	2:21	9:16	5:36
New wine	2:22	9:17	5:37
Rescued by a heretic (Samaritan)			10:30ff
Naive children		11:16	7:31-32
Divided kingdom overcome	3:23ff	12:25	11:17ff
Strong man disarmed	3:27	12:29	11:21
Yeast in the dough		13:33	13:20-21
Nagging friend			11:5ff
Nagging widow			18:1ff
Seed growing secretly	4:26ff		
Seed becoming a tree	4:30ff	13:31-32	13:18-19
Field of wheat and tares		13:24ff	
Net full of all sorts		13:47ff	
New treasures and old		13:52	
Workmen overpaid		20:1ff	
Preferred son		21:28ff	
Banquet for all		22:1ff	14:16ff
Lowest place at table			14:7ff
The poor as guests			14:12ff
One taken, one left		24:40-41	17:34-35
Burglar at night		24:42-43	12:39
Master at night	13:33ff	24:45	12:35
Bridegroom at night		25:1ff	
Preferred tax collector (Publican)			18:9ff

A challenge

	Mark	Matthew	Luke
Loss and gain	4:24-25	7:2, 13:12	6:38, 8:18, 19:26
Rich fool			12:16ff
Debtor in crisis		5:25	12:57ff
Barren fig tree			13:6ff
Tower builder			14:28ff
King going to war			14:31ff
Tasteless salt	9:49-50	5:13	14:34
Sound eye		6:22-23	11:34
One master		6:24	16:13
Splinters and planks		7:3ff	6:41-42
Narrow gate		7:13-14	13:24
Sound and rotten trees		7:16ff, 12:33	6:43-44
Rocky foundations		7:24ff	6:47ff
Employee under dismissal			16:1ff
Rich miser and Lazarus			16:19ff
Humble servant			17:7ff
Empty house		12:43ff	11:24ff
Reading the signs		16:2-3	12:54ff
Unforgiving servant		18:23ff	
Murderous vinedressers	12:1ff	21:33ff	20:9ff
Eagle and carcase		24:28	17:37
Money in trust		25:14ff	19:12ff
Sheep and goats		25:31	

The 1717 edition of the Authorised Version misprinted the headline of Luke 20 as 'The Husbandmen and the Vinegar'. It was known as the Vinegar Bible.

'Most people are troubled by the Scripture passages they don't understand. I'm most troubled by the passages I do understand.' Mark Twain

SECTION THREE: MAPS

1. THE WORLD OF THE PATRIARCHS (GENESIS – JUDGES)

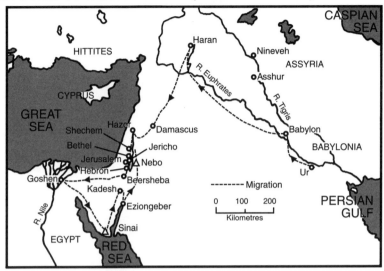

2. THE ISRAEL OF KINGS AND PROPHETS

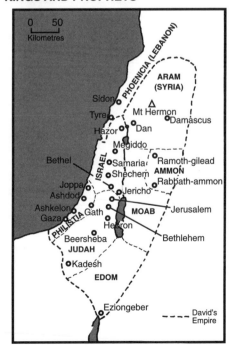

3. PALESTINE IN JESUS' TIME

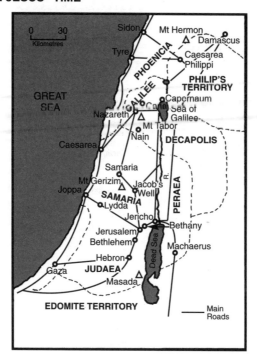

4. BIBLICAL JERUSALEM (present walls in dotted lines)

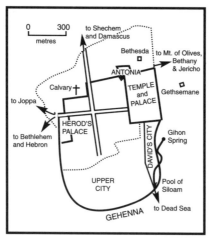

5. PAUL'S MISSIONARY JOURNEYS

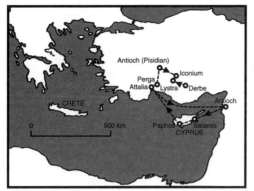

1st Journey
(Acts 13–14)

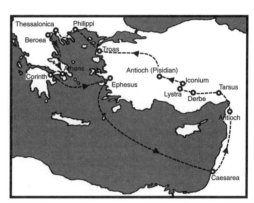

2nd Journey
(Acts 16–18)

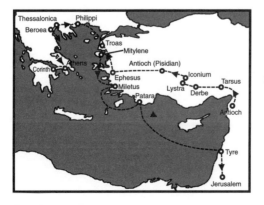

3rd Journey
(Acts 18–21)

SECTION FOUR: MISCELLANEOUS

1. Measurements in the Bible

Linear

Apart from the reed, the Old Testament measurements are based upon parts of the body. A cubit is the length of the forearm, a span the distance between the extended thumb and little finger, a hand the width of the palm, and a finger the breadth of the thumb. The fathom, furlong and mile are New Testament measurements.

	Modern equivalent	Value in cubits
mile	1.5km	3,200
furlong (stadion)	200m	400
reed	3m	6
fathom	2m	4
cubit	48cm	1
span	24cm	1/2
hand	8cm	1/6
finger	2cm	1/24

Liquid

	Modern equivalent in litres	Value in baths
cor	450	10
bath, measure	45	1
hin	7.5	1/6
kab	2.5	1/18
log	0.5	1/90

Dry

	Modern equivalent in litres	Value in ephahs
homer, cor	450	10
ephah	45	1
measure	15	1/3
tenth	5	1/10
kab	2.5	1/20

Weight

	Modern equivalent	Value in shekels
talent	35kg	3,500
mina, pound	500g	50
shekel	10g	1
half-shekel, drachma	5g	1/2
gerah	0.5g	1/20

Money

Many of the biblical money values were estimated by weight. These values are here given in silver: the same weights in gold were worth thirteen times as much. No attempt has been made to give any equivalent in modern coinage, because of its constantly changing value. But this may be estimated from the fact that the silver denarius, here used as a standard, was a day's wage for an unskilled labourer (see Matthew 20:2).

	Value in denarii
talent	12,000
mina, pound	200
shekel, silver piece	4
denarius, drachma, daric	1
penny	1/16
copper coin	1/64

Time

In the Old Testament, days were reckoned as beginning at sunset, not midnight. The night which followed was divided up into three watches of four hours each. Daytime was then similarly divided into three parts, called simply morning, noon and evening.

The New Testament uses the Roman division of the day, into four periods of three hours each, beginning with 6am. Midday was therefore known as the sixth hour.

Months were reckoned by the moon, and consisted of 29-30 days each. Their names were as follows:

First or Nisan or Abib	March - April
Second or Ziv	April - May
Third or Sivan	May - June
Fourth	June - July
Fifth	July - August
Sixth or Elul	August - September
Seventh or Ethanim	September - October
Eighth or Bul	October - November
Ninth or Chislev	November - December
Tenth or Tebeth	December - January
Eleventh or Shebat	January - February
Twelfth or Adar	February - March

The smallest edition of the Bible was the Mite Bible, published by the Oxford University Press in 1896. It measured 3.5 x 2.5 x 1 cm.

2. Symbolic numbers in the Bible

In common with many ancient writings, the Bible often uses numbers in a symbolic rather than a literal sense. Listed below are the meanings behind some of these numbers.

Three and a half
See under *Seven* below.

Four
Four often refers to the four directions (in front, behind, left and right), and therefore suggests fullness and totality. Thus four winds blow across the world (Jeremiah 49:36), Paradise is the source of four rivers which irrigate the whole earth (Genesis 2:10), the whole of history can be described in terms of four kingdoms (Daniel 2:36-40 and 7:17), God is enthroned on four living creatures (Ezekiel 1 and Revelation 4), and so on.

Six
See under *Seven* below.

Seven
Many aspects of the natural world come in sevens: seven colours of the rainbow, seven tones in the scale, seven planets known to the ancient world, seven sense organs in the head (eyes, ears, nostrils, mouth), seven days for each quarter of the moon, and so on. This probably explains why the Bible often uses the number seven as *the* supremely round number, indicating maximum completeness, whether for good or evil: there are seven petitions in the Lord's Prayer (Matthew 6:9f); forgiveness is to be given not only seven times but prodigally seventy times seven times (Matthew 18:22); the Magdalen is possessed by seven demons (Mark 16:9). The book of Revelation uses the number endlessly (seven churches, seven lamps, seven seals and so on) and this usage no doubt influenced the medieval numbering of the Christian sacraments as seven.

If seven means perfection, then six indicates the failure to reach perfection (the apocalyptic Beast's number is superlatively 666 in Revelation 13:18, see further below); and the number three-and-a-half suggests the fatally flawed and limited time in which persecutors have their own way (see for example Daniel 7:25, Revelation 12:14).

Eight
Because *seven* means perfection, the number eight suggests super-perfection (if such is possible). The eighth day after the seven days of creation would then be seen as the beginning of a new creation (Christian fonts were deliberately eight-sided). This new creation was made available by Jesus, whose name 'significantly' adds up to 888 (see page 31).

Ten

Ten is again a round number, based (like the decimal system) on the ten fingers of human hands. Like the number seven, it suggests totality and fullness, as in the Ten Plagues (Exodus 7-12) and the Ten Commandments (Exodus 20).

Twelve

Some of the ancients used a duodecimal (rather than decimal) system, based on the number twelve to be found in the zodiacal signs and in the months of the year. Hence the unit we still call a dozen, and the establishment of twelve prefectures by King Solomon (1 Kings 4:7), twelve tribes of Israel (Genesis 35:23) and twelve apostles (Mark 3:14).

Forty

Forty years is the biblical round number for a generation, a lifetime. Saul, David and Solomon are all described as reigning for forty years (Acts 13:21; 2 Samuel 5:4; 1 Kings 11:42). Because this was the duration of Israel's journey through the desert to their homeland (Deuteronomy 29:5), the number took on the overtones of a time of preparation before reaching the goal. Hence the forty days' rain which caused the Flood (Genesis 7:4), Elijah's forty days' march to the mountain of God (1 Kings 19:8), and Jesus' forty days in the desert before beginning his ministry (Mark 1:13). His resurrection appearances are also said to have lasted forty days (Acts 1:3).

Seventy

Seventy is, of course, the product of the two round numbers seven and ten. Like them (only more so) it is used to give an idea of totality and universality. So there are seventy descendants of Noah who repopulate the world after the flood (Genesis 10), seventy descendants of Israel to sojourn in Egypt (Genesis 46:27), seventy elders appointed to govern Israel (Numbers 11:16) and seventy disciples sent out by Jesus to preach the Gospel (Luke 10:1).

One thousand

One thousand and its multiples is used in the Bible to signify a fabulously large number (in Egyptian hieroglyphs the number is represented by a man holding up both hands as if to say, 'who can count that far?'). So the thousand years (or millennium) in Revelation 20 is the period both of Satan's defeat and of the endless enjoyment of victory by the faithful. Rebekah at her marriage to Isaac has ten thousand children wished on her (Genesis 24:60), and David ten thousand defeated enemies (1 Samuel 18:7). It is interesting that in Revelation 7 the persecuted faithful who are promised victory and salvation are alternately described as countless (verse 9) and as 144,000 (verse 4). The number is not real but symbolic. Such a large number simply is countless. 144 is the number twelve, squared to give a sense of completeness. And twelve is the number of the tribes of Israel (they are explicitly listed here), symbolic of the New Israel which is the Christian Church.

Letters as numbers

Some numbers in the Bible arise out of the fact that in Hebrew and Greek there are no separate symbols for numbers, so that letters of the alphabet have to be used instead (for example ABED = 1254, BABE = 2125). This means that any word or name can also be represented by its numerical value.

This seems to be the case in the book of Genesis, where Abraham's body-guard is referred to as Eliezer in 15:2, and as 318 men in 14:14 ('+L+Y+'+Z+R = 1+30+10+70+7+200 = 318).

Similarly the genealogy of Jesus in Matthew 1 is artificially presented in three lists of exactly fourteen names, because in Hebrew the name David (D+W+D = 4+6+4) adds up to fourteen. Jesus coming at the end of these 42 ancestors is therefore the beginning of the seventh seven, the perfect conclusion to the Davidic dynasty.

In Revelation 13:18, as noted above, the ferocious Beast persecuting the people of God is given the enigmatic number 666. Obviously many names can be made to add up to that figure (even Hitler has been suggested). But the name intended by the author seems to be the Roman Emperor Nero (AD 54-68), whose name in Hebrew (NRWN QSR = 50+200+6+50+100+60+200) adds up to 666. Since Christians were aware that Christ's name in Greek (IESOUS = 10+8+200+70+400+200) adds up to 888, transcending the perfection of 777 throughout, the name of Nero is being exposed as a laughable travesty, disastrously falling short of perfection again and again and again.

There is a delightful inscription in Pompeii which reads, 'I love the girl (who adds up to) 545'. Presumably both he and she knew who was meant, but no one else did.

When an English divine claimed that Napoleon Bonaparte was the apocalyptic beast referred to in Revelation 13:18 because his name, written in Arabic (leaving out only two letters) added up to 666, Lord Macaulay pointed out that his own name, written in Tamil, and leaving out the T in Thomas, the B in Babington and the M in Macaulay also adds up to 666. Not to mention the 658 members of the House of Commons, plus its three clerks, the Sergeant and his deputy, the Chaplain, the doorkeeper and the librarian.

3. Some traditional biblical lists

Three theological virtues
(1 Corinthians 13:13)

Faith
Hope
Charity

Three eminent good works
(Matthew 6:1-6, 16-18)

Prayer
Fasting
Almsdeeds

Four cardinal virtues
(Wisdom 8:7 and Greek
    philosophers)

Prudence
Justice
Fortitude
Temperance

Four last things
(Hebrews 9:27)

Death
Judgement
Hell
Heaven

Seven works of mercy
(Matthew 25:35f and Tobit 1:17f)

To feed the hungry
To give drink to the thirsty
To clothe the naked
To harbour the harbourless
To visit the sick
To visit the imprisoned
To bury the dead

Seven capital sins
(see Romans 1:29f and Galatians
    5:19f)

Pride
Covetousness
Lust
Anger
Gluttony
Envy
Sloth

Seven contrary virtues
(according to the Catholic
    Catechism)

Humility
Liberality
Chastity
Meekness
Temperance
Brotherly love
Diligence

Seven gifts of the Holy Spirit
(Isaiah 11:2f in the Latin Vulgate
    translation)

Wisdom
Understanding
Counsel
Fortitude
Knowledge
Piety
Fear of the Lord

Eight Beatitudes
(Matthew 5:3f)

Blessed are the poor in spirit, for theirs is the kingdom of heaven.

Blessed are the meek, for they shall possess the land.

Blessed are they that mourn, for they shall be comforted.

Blessed are they that hunger and thirst after justice, for they shall have their fill.

Blessed are the merciful, for they shall obtain mercy.

Blessed are the clean of heart, for they shall see God.

Blessed are the peacemakers, for they shall be called the children of God.

Blessed are they that suffer persecution for justice' sake, for theirs is the kingdom of heaven.

NB: Luke 6:20f reduces the Beatitudes to four by omitting the second, fifth, sixth and seventh; but brings the total number back to eight by adding Four Woes.

Ten Commandments
(Exodus 20, Deuteronomy 5)

	Catholic Numbering	Protestant Numbering
You shall have no other gods but me	1a	1
You shall not make any carved image	1b	2
You shall not misuse the name of Yahweh your God	2	3
Remember the Sabbath day and keep it holy	3	4
Honour your father and mother	4	5
You shall not commit murder	5	6
You shall not commit adultery	6	7
You shall not steal	7	8
You shall not bear false witness against your neighbour	8	9
You shall not covet your neighbour's wife	9	10a
You shall not covet your neighbour's goods	10	10b

Twelve fruits of the Holy Spirit
(Galatians 5:22)

Latin and Douay version	Greek and modern versions
Charity	Love
Joy	Joy
Peace	Peace
Patience	Patience
Benignity	Kindness
Goodness	Goodness
Longanimity	
Mildness	
Faith	Faithfulness
Modesty	Gentleness
Continency	Selfcontrol
Chastity	

Twelve tribes of Israel
(Genesis 49)

Reuben	Dan
Simeon	Gad
Levi	Asher
Judah	Naphtali
Zebulun	Joseph (= Ephraim and Manasseh)
Issachar	Benjamin

Twelve apostles
(Mark 3:16f)

Simon (Peter)	Matthew (Levi)
James	Thomas
John	James (the Less)
Andrew	Thaddaeus (Jude)
Philip	Simon
Bartholomew	Judas Iscariot

The 1631 edition of the Authorised Version omitted the 'not' from the seventh commandment in Exodus 20:14 so that it read: 'Thou shalt commit adultery.' It became known as the Wicked Bible.

4. Notable translations of the Bible into English

Date	Name of translation and comments/description
8th century	**Bede** translated parts of the Bible into Anglo-Saxon
950	**Anonymous.** Anglo-Saxon paraphrases in the margins of the seventh-century Latin Lindisfarne Gospels
1380	**John Wycliffe** from the Latin Bible
1525	**William Tyndale** from Hebrew and Greek
1535	**Miles Coverdale** revision
1537	**Thomas Matthew** revision
1539	**Great Bible**
1560	**Geneva Bible**
1568	**Bishops' Bible**
1582	**Rheims New Testament.** Catholic
1609	**Douay Bible.** Catholic
1611	**Authorised** or **King James Version**. This eventually superseded all previous translations
1750	**Bishop Challoner's** revision of Douay
1881-85	**Revised Version.** This failed to replace the Authorised
1901	**American Standard Version**
1903	**Richard Weymouth.** New Testament
1913-35	**Westminster Version.** Catholic, incomplete
1913-24	**James Moffatt**
1944-49	**Ronald Knox.** Catholic, translation from the Latin
1946-52	**Revised Standard Version** (Catholic edition 1966). This has largely inherited the supremacy of the Authorised Version
1958	**J. B. Phillips.** New Testament
1952	**E. V. Rieu.** New Testament
1961-70	**New English Bible** by scholars from all denominations
1965	**Amplified Bible.** USA
1966	**Jerusalem Bible.** Catholic, from original texts
1966-76	**Good News Bible**
1968-69	**William Barclay** New Testament
1970	**New American Bible.** Catholic
1971	**Living Bible.** USA
1971	**New American Standard Version**
1973-78	**New International Version**
1977-82	**New King James** or **Revised Authorised Version**
1985	**New Jerusalem Bible**
1988	**New Century Version**
1989	**Revised (New) English Bible**
1990	**New Revised Standard Version**
1995	**Contemporary English Version**
1996	**New Living** (Bible) **Translation**

When the fourteenth-century bishop of London offered to buy up all the remaining copies of John Wycliffe's translation of the Bible into English, in order to burn them ('It contains three thousand heresies and errors') Wycliffe was happy to co-operate in secret. The money enabled him to print a second, much improved, edition.

When the Revised Version of the New Testament was first published in 1881 by the Oxford Press, one million copies were sold on the first day.

5. Pronunciation of biblical names

N.B. Not all names have been included. Names omitted are those of which the pronunciation is obvious or already well known (for example Simon, Priscilla), and those which are too rare to merit an entry. In cases of doubt, the pronunciation advised by the *Revised Standard Version* has been followed.

Aaron	AIR-on	Ashkelon	ASH-kel-on
Abednego	a-BED-neg-o	Ashtaroth	ASH-ta-rōt
Abel	able	Asmodeus	as-MO-dee-us
Abiathar	a-BY-ath-er	Assyria	as-SI-ria
Abijah	a-BY-ja	Augustus	or-GUST-us
Abimelech	a-BIM-e-lek	Azariah	a-za-RY-a
Abinadab	a-BIN-a-dab		
Abiram	a-BY-ram	Baal	bail
Abishag	AB-ish-ag	Babel	BAY-ble
Absalom	AB-sa-lom	Balaam	BAY-lam
Aceldama	ak-EL-dam-a	Balak	BA-lak
Achaia	a-KY-ya	Barabbas	bar-AB-as
Adonijah	a-do-NY-ja	Barak	barrack
Adullam	a-DULL-am	Barsabbas	bar-SAB-as
Agabus	AG-a-bus	Bartimaeus	bar-tim-AY-us
Agag	AY-gag	Baruch	barruck
Agrippa	a-GRIP-a	Bashan	BAY-shan
Ahasuerus	a-has-WEAR-us	Bathsheba	bath-SHEE-ba
Ahaz	AY-haz	Beelzebub	bee-EL-zee-bub
Ahitophel	a-HIT-o-fel	Beersheba	beer-SHEE-ba
Ai	eye	Belial	BEE-lee-al
Akeldama	a-KEL-dam-a	Belshazzar	bel-SHAZ-ar
Alphaeus	al-FEE-us	Benaiah	ben-AI-a
Amalekites	a-MAL-ek-ites	Bethphage	BETH-fa-jee
Amaziah	a-ma-ZY-a	Bethsaida	beth-SAY-da
Ammonites	AM-on-ites	Beulah	BEW-la
Amnon	AM-non	Bilhah	BILL-ha
Amos	AY-moss	Bithynia	bith-IN-ya
Ananias	an-a-NY-as	Boanerges	bo-an-URGE-ees
Anathoth	AN-at-oth	Boaz	BO-az
Antioch	AN-tee-ok	Bozrah	BOZ-ra
Antipas	ANT-ip-as	Byblos	BIB-loss
Apollos	a-POLL-os		
Apollyon	a-POLL-ee-on	Caesar	SEES-er
Aquila	AK-wil-a	Caesarea	se-za-REE-a
Ararat	AR-a-rat	C. Philippi	S. FILL-ip-eye
Archelaus	ar-ke-LAY-us	Caiaphas	KY-ya-fas
Areopagus	a-ree-OP-a-gus	Cain	cane
Aristarchus	a-ris-TAR-kus	Caleb	KAY-leb
Armageddon	ar-ma-GED-on	Cana	KAY-na
Artaxerxes	ar-ta-ZERK-sees	Canaan(ite)	KAY-nan(ite)
Asa	AY-sa	Candace	KAN-da-kay
Asaph	AY-saf	Capernaum	ka-PER-nay-um
Ashdod	ASH-dōd	Caphtor	KAF-tor
Asher	ASH-er		

Cappadocia	ka-pa-DOSE-ya	Eutychus	YEW-tick-us
Carchemish	KAR-kem-ish	Exodus	EX-od-us
Cenchreae	KEN-kree-ay	Ezekiel	ez-EEK-yel
Cephas	SEE-fas or KAY-fas	Ezra	EZ-ra
Chedorlaomer	ked-or-la-O-mer		
Chemosh	KEE-mosh	Fortunatus	for-tew-NAY-tus
Cherethites &	KE-reth-ites &		
Pelethites	PE-leth-ites	Gabbatha	GAB-a-tha
Cherith	KER-ith	Gadara	GAD-a-ra
Chinnereth	KIN-er-eth	Galatia(ns)	gal-AY-sha(shuns)
Chorazin	kor-AD-zin	Gamaliel	ga-MAY-lee-el
Chusa	CHOO-sa	Gaza	GAH-za
Cleophas	KLEE-o-fas	Gehazi	ge-HAD-zi
Colossae	ko-LOSS-ay	Gehenna	ge-HEN-a
Colossians	ko-LOSH-ans	Genesis	JEN-e-sis
Cyrene	sy-REE-nee	Gennesareth	je-NES-a-reth
Cyrus	SY-rus	Gerar	JER-ar
		Gerasa	je-RA-sa
		Gerizim	JE-ri-zim
Dagon	DAY-gon	Gethsemani	geth-SEM-a-ni
Dalmanutha	dal-man-OOTH-a	Gezer	GAY-zer
Darius	da-RY-us	Gibeah	GIB-e-a
Delilah	de-LY-la	Gibeon	GIB-e-on
Derbe	DURB-ay	Gideon	GID-yon
Deuteronomy	dew-ter-RON-o-mee	Gihon	GI-hon
Dionysius	dy-on-IZZY-us	Gilboa	gil-BO-a
		Gilead	GIL-e-ad
Ebal	EE-bal	Gilgal	GIL-gal
Ebenezer	e-ben-EEZ-er	Golan	GO-lan
Ecclesiastes	ek-lees-ee-ASS-tees	Golgotha	GOL-goth-a
Ecclesiasticus	ek-lees-ee-ASS-tick-us	Goliath	go-LY-ath
Edom	EE-dom	Gomer	GO-mer
Elam	EE-lam	Gomorrah	go-MORR-a
Elath	AY-lat	Goshen	GO-shen
Eleazar	el-ee-AD-zar		
Eli	EE-lie	Habakkuk	ha-BACK-uk
Eliakim	e-LY-a-kim	Hagar	HAY-gar
Eliezer	e-li-ED-zer	Haggai	HAG-gay-eye
Elijah	e-LY-ja	Hakeldama	hak-EL-dam-a
Elim	EE-lim	Haman	HAY-man
Elimelech	e-LIM-e-lek	Hananiah	ha-na-NY-a
Eliphaz	El-i-faz	Havilah	HAV-il-a
Elisha	e-LY-sha	Hazael	HAZ-ail
Elkanah	el-KAHN-a	Hazor	HADS-or
Eloi	EL-o-ee	Heber	HEE-ber
Emmanuel	e-MAN-new-el	Hebron	HEE-bron
Emmaus	e-MAY-us	Heliodorus	hee-leo-DOR-us
Engedi	en-GED-I	Henoch	HEE-nok
Enoch	EE-nok	Hermes	HER-mees
Ephesians	e-FEE-shens	Herodias	her-O-di-as
Ephraim	EFF-rem	Hezekiah	he-ze-KY-a
Ephrathah	EFF-ra-tha	Hierapolis	higher-AP-o-lis
Esau	EE-saw	Hilkiah	hil-KY-a
Esdraelon	es-DREE-lon	Holofernes	ho-lo-FERN-ees
Euphrates	yew-FRAY-tes	Hosea	ho-SAY-a

37

Ichabod	IK-a-bod	Kibroth-	
Iconium	eye-KO-ni-um	hattavah	KIB-rote-ha-TA-a-va
Idumaea	id-yew-MEE-a	Kidron	KID-ron
Illyricum	il-IR-ik-um	Kirjath-jearim	KIR-yath-yay-a-
Immanuel	im-MAN-new-el		REEM
Isaac	EYE-zak	Kishon	KEE-shon
Isaiah	eye-ZY-a		
Iscariot	is-CARRY-ot		
Ishbaal	ISH-bail	Laban	LAY-ban
Ishbosheth	ish-BO-sheth	Lachish	LAY-kish
Ishmael	ISH-mail	Lamech	LAM-ek
Israel	IS-rail	Laodicia	lay-o-dis-EE-a
Issachar	ISS-a-kar	Leah	LAY-a
Ithamar	ITH-a-mar	Levi(tes)	LEE-vy(ts)
Ituraea	it-yew-REE-a	Leviathan	le-VY-a-than
		Leviticus	le-VIT-ic-us
		Lycaonia	ly-kay-OWN-ya
Jabbok	JAY-bok	Lysanias	ly-SAY-nee-as
Jabesh-Gilead	JAY-besh GIL-yad	Lysias	LIZ-ee-as
Jabin	JAY-bin		
Jael	jail		
Jair	JAY-ir	Maccabee	MAK-a-bee
Japheth	JAF-eth	Macedonia	mas-e-DO-nya
Jebus(ite)	JEE-bus(ite)	Machpela	mak-PAY-la
Jeduthun	jed-YEW-thun	Magog	MAY-gog
Jehoahaz	je-HO-ay-haz	Mahanaim	ma-ha-NAY-im
Jehoash	je-HO-ash	Maher-shalal-	
Jehoiachin	je-HOY-a-keen	hash-baz	MAY-her-SHAY-lal
Jehoiada	je-HOY-a-da		HASH-baz
Jehoiakim	je-HOY-a-keem	Malachi	MAL-a-ky
Jehoram	je-HOR-am	Mamre	MAM-ray
Jehoshaphat	je-HO-sha-fat	Manasseh	man-ASS-ay
Jehu	JEE-hew	Maranatha	mar-an-ATH-a
Jephthah	JEF-tha	Maresha	mar-AY-sha
Jeremiah	jer-e-MY-a	Mattathias	mat-ta-THY-as
Jeroboam	je-ro-BO-am	Matthias	ma-THY-as
Jerubaal	je-roo-BAIL	Megiddo	me-GID-do
Jesse	JESS-ay	Melchizedek	mel-KIZ-a-dek
Jethro	JETH-ro	Menahem	MEN-a-hem
Jezreel	JEZ-ree-el	Menelaus	men-e-LAY-us
Joab	JO-ab	Mephibosheth	me-FIB-o-sheth
Joash	JO-ash	Meribah	MERRY-ba
Job	Joe-b	Merodach-	
Jochebed	JOK-e-bed	baladan	me-RO-dak-BAL-a
Joel	JO-el		dan
Joshua	JOSH-yew-a	Meshach	MEE-shak
Josiah	jo-SY-a	Methuselah	me-THOOS-se-la
Jotham	JO-tham	Micah	MY-ka
Jubal	JEW-bal	Micaiah	mik-KY-ya
Judaea	jew-DEE-a	Midian	MID-yan
Judah	JEW-da	Miletus	my-LEET-us
Justus	JUST-us	Mitylene	mit-ty-LEE-nee
		Mordecai	MOR-de-ky
Kadesh Barnea	KAY-desh BARN-ya	Moresheth-gath	MOR-esh-eth-GATH
Kedar	KAY-dar	Moriah	mo-RY-a

Naaman	NAY-man	Pisgah	PIS-ga
Nabal	NAY-bal	Pishon	PEE-shon
Naomi	NAY-o-mee	Pisidia	py-SID-ya
Naphtali	NAF-ta-lee	Pithom	PY-thom
Nathanael	na-THAN-yel	Potiphar	POTTY-far
Nebo	NEE-bo	Praetorium	pre-TOR-ium
Nebuchad-		Prochorus	PROK-or-us
nezzar	ne-book-ad-NEDS-ar	Procurator	PRO-kew-ray-tor
Necho	NE-ko	Psalms	sarms
Nehemiah	nee-a-MY-a	Ptolemais	tol-e-MAY-is
Nicanor	ni-KAIN-or	Ptolemy	TOLL-e-mee
Nicodemus	ni-ko-DEEM-us	Purim	POOR-im
Nicopolis	nik-OP-o-lis	Puteoli	put-AY-o-lee
Niger	NY-jer		
Nineveh	NIN-ev-e	Quirinius	kwi-RIN-ee-us
Obadiah	o-ba-DY-a	Raamses	RAM-sees
Oholah	o-HO-la	Raguel	RAG-yew-el
Oholibah	o-HO-lib-a	Rahab	RAY-hab
Omri	OM-ree	Ramah	RA-ma
Onan	O-nan	Rameses	RAM-e-sees
Onesimus	on-ES-i-mus	Ramoth Gilead	RAY-moth GIL-e-ad
Onesiphorus	on-e-SIF-or-us	Raphael	RAF-ail
Onias	o-NY-as	Rebekah	re-BEK-a
Ophir	O-fir	Rechabites	REK-a-bites
Ophni	OFF-nee	Rehoboam	re-ho-BO-am
Ophrah	OFF-ra	Rephaim	re-FY-im
Orpah	OR-pa	Rephidim	REF-id-im
Osnappar	os-NAP-er	Reuben	ROO-ben
Othniel	OTH-nee-yel	Reuel	ROO-el
		Rezin	REZ-in
		Rhegium	RAY-jee-um
Paddan-aram	PAD-an-AY-ram		
Pamphylia	pam-FIL-ya		
Parmenas	PAR-men-as	Sabacthani	sa-bak-TA-nee
Pashur	PASH-hur	Sadducees	SAD-yew-sees
Pekah	PAY-ka	Salamis	SAL-a-mis
Pekahiah	pe-ka-HY-a	Salem	SAY-lem
Penuel	pe-NEW-el	Salim	SAY-lim
Pergamum	PER-gam-um	Salome	sa-LO-me
Perizzites	PERRY-zy-ts	Samaritans	sa-MARRY-tans
Persepolis	per-SEP-o-lis	Samothrace	SAM-o-thrayce
Pharaoh	FAIR-o	Sanballat	san-BAL-at
Pharisees	FARRY-sees	Saphira	sa-FY-ra
Philadelphia	fil-ad-ELF-ya	Sceva	SKAY-va
Philemon	fy-LEE-mon	Scythian	SITH-yan
Philetus	fy-LEE-tus	Seleucia	sel-YEW-see-a
Philippi	FIL-ip-eye	Seleucid	sel-YEW-sid
Philippians	fi-LIP-yans	Sennacherib	se-NAK-er-ib
Philistia	fi-LIST-ya	Sepharvaim	se-far-VAY-im
Philistines	FIL-ist-ines	Shadrach	SHAD-rack
Phinehas	FINE-ee-as	Shalisha	SHALL-ish-a
Phoebe	FEE-bee	Shallum	SHALL-um
Phoenicia	fe-NEESH-ya	Shalmaneser	shal-man-EES-er
Phrygia	FRIDGE-ya	Shealtiel	she-AL-ti-el

Shear-jashub	SHAY-ar-YASH-ub	Theudas	THEW-das
Sheba	SHEE-ba	Thummim	TOOM-im
Shechem	SHEK-em	Thyatira	thy-a-TY-ra
Shemaiah	she-MY-a	Tiberias(us)	ty-BEER-ee-as(us)
Sheol	SHAY-ol	Tiglath-pileser	TIG-lath py-LEES-er
Sheshbazzar	shesh-BAZ-ar	Tobijah	to-BY-ja
Sheva	SHEE-va	Trachonitis	track-o-NY-tis
Shibboleth	SHIB-o-leth	Trophimus	TRO-fim-us
Shiloh	SHY-lo	Tryphon	TRY-fon
Shimei	SHIM-e-eye	Tubalcain	tew-bal-KAIN
Shulammite	SHU-lam-ite	Tychicus	TICK-ik-us
Sidon	SY-don	Tyrannus	ty-RAN-us
Siloam	sy-LO-am		
Sinai	SY-nay-eye	Ur	er
Sisera	SIS-e-ra	Urbanus	er-BAY-nus
Smyrna	SMUR-na	Uriah	yew-RY-a
Sosipater	so-SIP-a-ter	Urim	YEW-rim
Sosthenes	SOS-the-nees	Uzzah	UDS-a
Stephanas	STEF-an-as	Uzziah	ud-ZY-a
Succoth	SUCK-ōth		
Sychar	SICK-ar	Vashti	VASH-tee
Syene	sy-EE-nee		
Synteche	SIN-tek-ee	Xerxes	ZER-sees
Syrophoenician	SY-ro-fen-EE-shen		
Syrtis	SER-tis	Yahweh	YA-way
Taanach	TAR-nak	Zacchaeus	za-KEE-us
Tabeel	TAB-ee-el	Zacharias	zak-a-RY-as
Taberah	TAB-er-a	Zadok	ZAY-dok
Tabitha	TAB-ith-a	Zalmunna	zal-MUNN-a
Talitha cumi	TAL-ith-a KOO-mi	Zaphenath-	
Tarshish	TAR-shish	paneah	ZAF-en-ath pa-NAY-a
Tattenai	TAT-en-eye	Zarephath	ZAR-ef-ath
Tekoa	te-KO-a	Zarethan	ZAR-eth-an
Telabib	tel-a-BEEB	Zebedee	ZEB-ed-ee
Terah	TAY-ra	Zebulun	ZEB-yew-lun
Teraphim	TER-a-fim	Zechariah	ze-ka-RY-a
Tertius	TER-shus	Zedekiah	ze-de-KY-a
Tertullus	ter-TULL-us	Zeeb	ZAY-eb
Thaddaeus	thad-EE-us	Zephaniah	ze-fa-NY-a
Thebes	THEEbs	Zerubbabel	ze-RUB-a-bel
Thebez	THEB-ez	Zeruiah	zer-yew-EYE-a
Theophilus	the-O-fil-us	Zeus	z-YOOS
Thessalonians	thess-a-LO-nee-ans	Zipporah	ZIP-or-a
Thessalonika	thess-a-LON-ik-a		

> *The vision described in the opening pages of the book of Ezekiel was said by the rabbis to be beyond human powers to visualise, and they forbade it to be read by anyone under thirty.*